MEDICAL ERRORS

TABLE OF CONTENTS

INTRODUCTION

Medical errors represent a critical concern within the healthcare industry, posing substantial risks to patient safety and resulting in significant financial costs. Despite advancements in medical technology and increased awareness, the occurrence of medical errors remains alarmingly high. The purpose of this book, "Mastering Medical Errors: A Comprehensive Guide for Healthcare Providers," is to provide an in-depth understanding of medical errors, their causes, and effective strategies for prevention.

Medical errors can occur at any stage of patient care, from diagnosis to treatment and follow-up. They can result from a variety of factors, including miscommunication, human error, and system failures. The complexity of the healthcare environment further exacerbates the potential for errors, making it imperative for healthcare providers to be well-informed and proactive in their approach to patient safety.

This book is designed to be both informative and engaging, aiming to equip healthcare providers with the knowledge and tools necessary to identify, report, and prevent medical errors. Through a comprehensive exploration of the topic, readers will gain insights into the underlying causes of errors, the importance of effective communication, the role of technology, and the ethical and legal implications involved.

By the end of this book, healthcare providers will have a comprehensive understanding of medical errors and be equipped with practical tools to enhance patient safety. The goal is to foster a proactive approach to error prevention, ultimately leading to improved patient outcomes and a safer healthcare environment.

MODULE ONE

LESSON ONE: MEDICAL ERRORS

Medical errors are unintended acts, omissions, or deviations from accepted practices that can cause harm to patients. These errors encompass a wide range of issues, including diagnostic errors, medication errors, surgical errors, and system failures. Understanding the scope and impact of medical errors is the first step toward addressing this pervasive problem.

The historical context of medical errors dates back to ancient times, but it wasn't until the late 20th century that the issue gained significant attention. In 1999, the Institute of Medicine (IOM) released a landmark report titled "To Err Is Human: Building a Safer Health System," which estimated that between 44,000 and 98,000 Americans die each year due to preventable medical errors. This report galvanized the healthcare community and policymakers, leading to increased efforts to improve patient safety.

Medical errors can occur in various forms and at different stages of patient care. Diagnostic errors involve missed, delayed, or incorrect diagnoses, often resulting from cognitive biases, inadequate information, or miscommunication. Medication errors include prescribing the wrong medication, incorrect dosages, or administration mistakes. Surgical errors encompass wrong-site surgery, retained surgical instruments, and other intraoperative mistakes. System failures refer to issues within healthcare processes, such as poor coordination, inadequate staffing, or faulty equipment.

The impact of medical errors is profound, affecting patients, families, and healthcare providers. For patients, errors can lead to physical harm, prolonged hospital stays, increased medical costs, and emotional distress. Families may experience grief, financial burdens, and a loss of trust in the healthcare system. Healthcare providers involved in errors may suffer from guilt, stress, and professional repercussions. Additionally, medical errors contribute to significant economic costs, estimated to be in the billions of dollars annually in the United States alone.

Addressing medical errors requires a multifaceted approach. It involves not only understanding the causes and types of errors but also implementing strategies for prevention and fostering a culture of safety within healthcare organizations. Education and training play a crucial role in equipping healthcare providers with the skills and knowledge needed to identify and mitigate errors. Continuous improvement and learning from past mistakes are essential components of an effective patient safety program.

MODULE TWO

LESSON ONE: UNDERSTANDING THE CAUSES OF MEDICAL ERRORS

Medical errors are multifaceted, resulting from a complex interplay of various factors. To effectively address and prevent these errors, it is crucial to understand their root causes. This lesson explores the primary contributors to medical errors, categorized into individual, system, and environmental factors, and discusses how each can be mitigated.

INDIVIDUAL FACTORS

Individual factors pertain to the characteristics and behaviors of healthcare providers that can lead to medical errors. These include cognitive biases, knowledge deficits, skill limitations, and psychological factors.

1. Cognitive Biases

Cognitive biases are systematic patterns of deviation from norm or rationality in judgment. In healthcare, they can significantly impact diagnostic accuracy. Common cognitive biases include:

- Confirmation Bias: The tendency to search for, interpret, and remember information that confirms one's preconceptions, leading to diagnostic errors.
- Anchoring Bias: The reliance on the first piece of information encountered (the "anchor") when making decisions, which can result in misdiagnosis.
- Availability Heuristic: Overestimating the likelihood of events based on their availability in memory, often influenced by recent exposure to similar cases.

2. Knowledge Deficits

Knowledge deficits can arise from inadequate education, insufficient training, or lack of experience. These deficits can lead to errors in:

- Diagnosis: Misinterpretation of clinical signs, symptoms, and test results.
- Treatment: Incorrect selection of therapeutic interventions.
- Medication Administration: Errors in dosing, route, or selection of medications.

3. Skill Limitations

Skill limitations involve deficiencies in technical proficiency and decision-making abilities. These can manifest as:

- Technical Errors: Mistakes made during procedures or use of medical devices.
- Decision-Making Errors: Poor clinical judgments due to inadequate critical thinking skills.

PSYCHOLOGICAL FACTORS

Psychological factors such as stress, fatigue, and burnout can significantly affect a healthcare provider's performance. These factors can lead to reduced attention, impaired judgment, and increased likelihood of errors.

SYSTEM FACTORS

System factors encompass the organizational and process-related aspects of healthcare delivery that can contribute to errors. These include communication failures, inadequate staffing, workflow inefficiencies, and poor system design.

Communication Failures

Effective communication is vital for patient safety. Communication failures can occur between:

- Healthcare Teams: Misunderstandings and incomplete information transfer can result in errors in patient care.
- Providers and Patients: Inadequate communication with patients can lead to misunderstandings about treatment plans, medication instructions, and follow-up care.

Inadequate Staffing and Workload

Staffing shortages and high workload can overwhelm healthcare providers, leading to:

- Fatigue: Overworked and fatigued providers are more prone to errors.
- Burnout: Chronic stress and burnout can reduce job performance and increase the risk of mistakes.

Workflow Inefficiencies

Inefficient workflows can create opportunities for errors. Examples include:

- Poorly Designed Processes: Inconsistent procedures and lack of standardization can lead to variability in care.
- Inadequate Policies: Absence of clear guidelines and protocols can result in errors due to improvisation and lack of direction.

System Design Flaws

Flaws in system design, such as faulty equipment or poorly designed healthcare facilities, can contribute to errors. Issues include:

- Equipment Malfunctions: Faulty or unreliable medical equipment can lead to diagnostic and treatment errors.
- Facility Layout: Poorly organized or cluttered workspaces can increase the likelihood of misplacing or misidentifying equipment and medications.

ENVIRONMENTAL FACTORS

Environmental factors refer to the physical and organizational setting in which healthcare is provided. These factors include the work environment, the availability of resources, and the overall organizational culture.

Work Environment

The work environment can significantly impact the performance of healthcare providers. Factors include:

- Noise and Distractions: High noise levels and frequent interruptions can disrupt concentration and increase the risk of errors.
- Lighting and Ergonomics: Poor lighting and ergonomically unfriendly workspaces can impair performance and contribute to mistakes.

Availability of Resources

The availability and reliability of resources are crucial for safe and effective healthcare delivery. Factors impacting resource availability include:

- Medical Supplies: Shortages of essential medical supplies can lead to the use of substitutes or rationing, increasing the risk of errors.
- Staff Support: Adequate support from other healthcare staff, such as nurses and allied health professionals, is necessary to ensure comprehensive patient care.

Organizational Culture

The culture of a healthcare organization significantly influences the occurrence of medical errors. Key aspects of organizational culture that affect patient safety include:

- Leadership: Leaders play a critical role in establishing and promoting a culture of safety. Their commitment to patient safety sets the tone for the entire organization.
- Transparency: An open and transparent culture encourages reporting of errors and near misses, facilitating learning and improvement.
- Continuous Improvement: A culture that prioritizes continuous improvement and learning from mistakes is essential for reducing medical errors.

HUMAN FACTORS ENGINEERING

Human factors engineering is an interdisciplinary field focused on improving the interaction between humans and other elements of a system. In healthcare, this involves designing systems and processes that enhance human performance and minimize the likelihood of errors. Key principles of human factors engineering include:

- User-Centered Design: Designing medical devices, healthcare facilities, and workflows with the end-user in mind to ensure they are intuitive and easy to use.
- Standardization: Standardizing processes and procedures to reduce variability and improve reliability.
- Ergonomics: Ensuring that work environments are ergonomically designed to reduce physical strain and improve performance.

MODULE THREE

LESSON ONE: RECOGNIZING AND REPORTING MEDICAL ERRORS

Recognizing and reporting medical errors is a critical step in improving patient safety and fostering a culture of transparency and accountability within healthcare organizations. This lesson will explore the importance of identifying medical errors, the methods for recognizing them, and the best practices for reporting errors to facilitate learning and prevention.

The Importance of Recognizing Medical Errors

Medical errors can have serious consequences for patients, healthcare providers, and the healthcare system as a whole. Recognizing these errors is essential for several reasons:

- Patient Safety: Prompt identification of errors can prevent further harm to patients and allow for timely corrective actions.
- Quality Improvement: Understanding the nature and frequency of errors can inform quality improvement initiatives and lead to the development of safer practices and protocols.
- Accountability: Recognizing errors helps establish accountability within healthcare organizations, encouraging providers to adhere to best practices and standards.
- Learning Opportunities: Errors provide valuable opportunities for learning and education, helping healthcare providers to avoid similar mistakes in the future.

METHODS FOR RECOGNIZING MEDICAL ERRORS

Healthcare providers can use various methods to recognize medical errors, including:

Incident Reporting Systems

Incident reporting systems are structured tools that allow healthcare providers to document and report errors and near misses. These systems typically include:

- Online Portals: Secure web-based platforms where providers can submit reports.
- Paper Forms: Traditional paper-based reporting forms that can be completed and submitted manually.
- Hotlines: Dedicated phone lines for reporting errors anonymously or confidentially.

Incident reporting systems should be easy to use, accessible, and encourage voluntary reporting without fear of retribution.

Chart Audits and Reviews

Chart audits and reviews involve systematic examination of patient records to identify errors. This method can be used to:

- Identify Patterns: Detect recurring issues or trends that may indicate systemic problems.
- Verify Compliance: Ensure adherence to established protocols and guidelines.
- Assess Outcomes: Evaluate the outcomes of care and identify areas for improvement.

Regular chart audits and reviews are essential for ongoing monitoring and quality assurance.

Root Cause Analysis (RCA)

Root cause analysis is a structured approach to identifying the underlying causes of errors. RCA involves:

- Data Collection: Gathering information about the error, including timelines, involved personnel, and contributing factors.
- Cause Mapping: Creating a visual representation of the error's causes and their relationships.
- Identification of Root Causes: Determining the fundamental issues that led to the error.
- Development of Action Plans: Creating strategies to address and mitigate the root causes.

RCA is a powerful tool for understanding complex errors and implementing effective corrective actions.

Failure Mode and Effects Analysis (FMEA)

Failure mode and effects analysis is a proactive method for identifying potential errors before they occur. FMEA involves:

- Identifying Failure Modes: Listing possible ways a process or system can fail.
- Assessing Effects: Evaluating the potential impact of each failure mode on patient safety.
- Prioritizing Risks: Ranking the failure modes based on their severity, likelihood, and detectability.
- Developing Mitigation Strategies: Creating plans to reduce the risk of failure and its impact.

FMEA helps healthcare organizations anticipate and prevent errors by addressing vulnerabilities in their systems and processes.

Direct Observation

Direct observation involves monitoring healthcare processes and provider-patient interactions in real-time to identify errors. This method can be used to:

- Detect Deviations: Identify deviations from established protocols and guidelines.

- Assess Competence: Evaluate the skills and performance of healthcare providers.
- Improve Training: Inform the development of targeted training programs to address identified gaps.

Direct observation is particularly useful in high-risk areas, such as surgery and medication administration.

MODULE FOUR

LESSON ONE: STRATEGIES FOR PREVENTING MEDICAL ERRORS

Preventing medical errors requires a comprehensive approach that addresses the multifaceted nature of healthcare delivery. This lesson outlines effective strategies for minimizing errors, focusing on system redesign, process improvement, staff education, technology integration, and fostering a culture of safety.

SYSTEM REDESIGN

System redesign involves modifying existing healthcare systems to reduce the likelihood of errors. Key strategies include:

Standardization of Processes

Standardizing processes helps ensure consistency and reliability in patient care. This can be achieved by:

- Developing Protocols and Guidelines: Creating clear, evidence-based protocols and guidelines for common procedures and treatments.
- Implementing Checklists: Using checklists to ensure that all necessary steps are completed during medical procedures, such as surgical safety checklists.
- Standardizing Medication Administration: Standardizing medication labeling, packaging, and administration procedures to minimize errors.

Simplifying Workflows

Simplifying workflows can reduce complexity and the potential for errors. Strategies include:

- Streamlining Tasks: Eliminating unnecessary steps and redundancies in care processes.
- Improving Information Flow: Ensuring that critical information is easily accessible and flows seamlessly between healthcare providers.
- Reducing Hand-offs: Minimizing the number of hand-offs and transitions of care, which are high-risk points for errors.

PROCESS IMPROVEMENT

Continuous process improvement is essential for identifying and mitigating risks. Key methods include:

Lean Six Sigma

Lean Six Sigma combines lean manufacturing principles with Six Sigma methodologies to improve efficiency and reduce variability in healthcare processes. This involves:

- Identifying Waste: Eliminating wasteful activities that do not add value to patient care.
- Reducing Variation: Standardizing processes to reduce variation and improve predictability.
- Implementing PDCA Cycles: Using Plan-Do-Check-Act (PDCA) cycles to test and refine process improvements.

Root Cause Analysis (RCA)

Conducting RCA after errors occur helps identify underlying causes and develop corrective actions. This process includes:

- Data Collection: Gathering detailed information about the error, including timelines, involved personnel, and contributing factors.
- Cause Mapping: Creating visual diagrams to illustrate the relationships between different causes.

- Developing Action Plans: Implementing targeted interventions to address identified root causes.

Failure Mode and Effects Analysis (FMEA)

FMEA is a proactive tool used to identify and mitigate potential errors before they occur. This involves:

- Identifying Failure Modes: Listing possible ways a process or system can fail.
- Assessing Risk: Evaluating the potential impact, likelihood, and detectability of each failure mode.
- Prioritizing Interventions: Focusing on high-risk areas and developing strategies to mitigate potential failures.

STAFF EDUCATION AND TRAINING

Continuous education and training for healthcare providers are critical for preventing medical errors. Key initiatives include:

Simulation-Based Training

Simulation-based training provides hands-on experience in a controlled environment, allowing healthcare providers to practice and refine their skills without risking patient safety. Benefits include:

- Enhancing Clinical Skills: Practicing complex procedures and emergency responses.
- Improving Teamwork: Developing communication and collaboration skills within healthcare teams.
- Building Confidence: Providing a safe space for providers to learn from mistakes and build confidence in their abilities.

Cognitive Bias Awareness

Educating healthcare providers about cognitive biases can help them recognize and mitigate these biases in clinical decision-making. Strategies include:

- Training Programs: Offering workshops and training sessions on cognitive bias awareness and decision-making.
- Decision Support Tools: Implementing tools that prompt providers to consider alternative diagnoses and treatments.

Continuing Medical Education (CME)

Regular CME programs ensure that healthcare providers stay current with the latest evidence-based practices and advancements in their field. Components include:

- Online Courses: Providing access to online courses and webinars on patient safety and error prevention.
- Workshops and Conferences: Encouraging participation in workshops and conferences focused on improving clinical skills and patient safety.

TECHNOLOGY INTEGRATION

Leveraging technology can significantly reduce the risk of medical errors. Key technologies include:

Electronic Health Records (EHRs)

EHRs improve the accuracy and accessibility of patient information, reducing the likelihood of errors. Benefits include:

- Comprehensive Patient Data: Providing a centralized repository of patient information, including medical history, medications, and allergies.
- Clinical Decision Support: Offering alerts and reminders for potential drug interactions, allergies, and other risks.

- Enhanced Communication: Facilitating seamless communication and information sharing among healthcare providers.

Computerized Physician Order Entry (CPOE)

CPOE systems allow healthcare providers to enter and manage orders electronically, reducing errors associated with handwritten orders. Advantages include:

- Error Reduction: Minimizing transcription errors and illegibility issues.
- Standardized Ordering: Ensuring consistent and accurate ordering processes.
- Real-Time Alerts: Providing real-time alerts for potential errors, such as drug interactions or contraindications.

Barcode Medication Administration (BCMA)

BCMA systems use barcode technology to verify patient identity and medication details before administration. Benefits include:

- Accurate Medication Administration: Ensuring the correct medication is given to the right patient at the right dose and time.
- Documentation: Automatically recording medication administration in the EHR.
- Error Alerts: Providing alerts for potential errors, such as wrong medication or dose.

MODULE FIVE

LESSON ONE: THE IMPACT OF TECHNOLOGY ON MEDICAL ERROR PREVENTION

Technology has revolutionized healthcare, providing tools and systems that significantly enhance patient safety and reduce the incidence of medical errors. This lesson explores the various technological advancements that have transformed healthcare practices, focusing on electronic health records (EHRs), computerized physician order entry (CPOE), clinical decision support systems (CDSS), telemedicine, and artificial intelligence (AI).

Electronic Health Records (EHRs)

EHRs are digital versions of patients' paper charts, offering a comprehensive, real-time record of patient information accessible to authorized users across different healthcare settings. The implementation of EHRs has had a profound impact on reducing medical errors through:

Improved Accessibility and Continuity of Care

Centralized Information: EHRs provide a single, comprehensive source of patient information, including medical history, medications, allergies, and test results, ensuring that all healthcare providers have access to up-to-date information.

- Continuity of Care: EHRs facilitate the seamless transfer of patient information between different providers and care settings, reducing the risk of information gaps and errors during transitions of care.

Enhanced Documentation and Legibility

- Elimination of Handwriting Errors: Digital documentation eliminates issues related to illegible handwriting, a common source of medication and treatment errors.
- Standardized Data Entry: EHRs use standardized templates and fields, ensuring consistent and accurate data entry.

Clinical Decision Support

- Alerts and Reminders: EHRs can integrate CDSS, providing alerts and reminders for potential drug interactions, allergies, and other critical patient safety issues.
- Evidence-Based Guidelines: EHRs can embed evidence-based guidelines and protocols, helping providers make informed clinical decisions.

Computerized Physician Order Entry (CPOE)

- CPOE systems allow healthcare providers to enter medical orders electronically, reducing errors associated with handwritten orders. Key benefits of CPOE include:

Reduction of Medication Errors

- Error-Free Orders: Electronic entry eliminates transcription errors and issues related to illegible handwriting.
- Decision Support: CPOE systems can provide real-time alerts for potential medication errors, such as incorrect dosages, drug interactions, and contraindications.

Standardization and Efficiency

- Standardized Ordering: CPOE systems standardize the ordering process, ensuring consistency and accuracy.
- Efficiency: Electronic orders are processed more quickly than paper orders, reducing delays in patient care.

Monitoring and Analytics

- Data Analytics: CPOE systems enable the collection and analysis of order data, identifying trends and areas for improvement.
- Compliance Monitoring: Systems can monitor adherence to clinical guidelines and protocols, enhancing quality of care.

CLINICAL DECISION SUPPORT SYSTEMS (CDSS)

CDSS are integrated with EHRs and CPOE systems to provide real-time support to healthcare providers. These systems enhance patient safety by:

Providing Real-Time Alerts and Reminders

- Medication Alerts: CDSS can alert providers to potential drug interactions, allergies, and contraindications.
- Diagnostic Support: Systems can suggest possible diagnoses based on patient data, helping providers consider all relevant possibilities.

Guiding Evidence-Based Practices

- Protocols and Guidelines: CDSS can embed clinical guidelines and protocols, ensuring that care is based on the latest evidence.
- Best Practices: Systems can recommend best practices for managing specific conditions, improving patient outcomes.

Enhancing Diagnostic Accuracy

- Decision Trees and Algorithms: CDSS can use decision trees and algorithms to assist providers in making accurate diagnoses.
- Reducing Cognitive Bias: By providing objective data and recommendations, CDSS can help reduce cognitive biases in clinical decision-making.

Technology has become an integral part of healthcare, offering powerful tools to enhance patient safety and reduce medical errors. EHRs, CPOE systems, CDSS, telemedicine, and AI have all contributed to more accurate, efficient, and safer healthcare delivery. By leveraging these technologies, healthcare organizations can significantly improve patient outcomes and minimize the risk

CONCLUSION

Preventing medical errors is a complex and multifaceted challenge that requires a comprehensive and systematic approach. This book has explored various dimensions of medical errors, from understanding their causes to implementing strategies for prevention, enhancing communication, leveraging technology, and fostering a culture of safety within healthcare organizations.

Preventing medical errors is an ongoing journey that requires the dedication and collaboration of healthcare providers, organizations, patients, and policymakers. By understanding the complexities of medical errors and implementing comprehensive prevention strategies, the healthcare community can create safer environments, improve patient outcomes, and build a more resilient and effective healthcare system.

This book serves as a guide for healthcare providers, offering insights and practical strategies to enhance patient safety. Together, we can make significant strides in reducing medical errors and ensuring that every patient receives the highest quality of care.

REFERENCES

- Berwick, D. M. (2003). *"Improvement, trust, and the healthcare workforce." Quality and Safety in Health Care.*
- Brennan, T. A., Leape, L. L., Laird, N. M., Hebert, L., Localio, A. R., Lawthers, A. G., ... & *Hiatt, H. H. (1991). "Incidence of adverse events and negligence in hospitalized patients: Results of the Harvard Medical Practice Study I." New England Journal of Medicine.*
- Carayon, P., Hundt, A. S., Karsh, B. T., Gurses, A. P., Alvarado, C. J., Smith, M., & Brennan, P. F. (2006). *"Work system design for patient safety: The SEIPS model." Quality and Safety in Health Care.*
- Classen, D. C., Resar, R., Griffin, F., Federico, F., Frankel, T., Kimmel, N & James, B. C. (2011). *"'Global Trigger Tool' shows that adverse events in hospitals may be ten times greater than previously measured." Health Affairs.*
- Donaldson, M. S., Corrigan, J. M., & Kohn, L. T. (Eds.). (2000). *To Err is Human: Building a Safer Health System. National Academies Press.*
- Gandhi, T. K., Berwick, D. M., & Shojania, K. G. (2002). *"Patient safety at the crossroads." Journal of the American Medical Association.*
- Institute of Medicine (IOM). (2001). *Crossing the Quality Chasm: A New Health System for the 21st Century. National Academy Press.*
- James, J. T. (2013). *"A new, evidence-based estimate of patient harms associated with hospital care." Journal of Patient Safety.*
- Kohn, L. T., Corrigan, J. M., & Donaldson, M. S. (Eds.). (2000). *To Err is Human: Building a Safer Health System. National Academy Press.*